ACHIEVING FINANCIAL FREEDOM FOR TEENAGERS.

SERIES:
FINANCIAL FREEDOM AT ANY AGE.

ACHIEVING FINANCIAL FREEDOM FOR TEENAGERS

Series "Financial Freedom at Any Age"
By: D.K. Hawkins
Version 1.1 ~December 2021
Published by D.K. Hawkins at KDP
Copyright ©2021 by D.K. Hawkins. All rights reserved.

No part of this publication may be reproduced, distributed or transmitted in any form or by any means including photocopying, recording or other electronic or mechanical methods or by any information storage or retrieval system without the prior written permission of the publishers, except in the case of very brief quotations embodied in critical reviews and certain other noncommercial uses permitted by copyright law.

All rights reserved, including the right of reproduction in whole or in part in any form.

All information in this book has been carefully researched and checked for factual accuracy. However, the author and publisher make no warranty, express or implied, that the information contained herein is appropriate for every individual, situation, or purpose and assume no responsibility for errors or omissions.

The reader assumes the risk and full responsibility for all actions. The author will not be held responsible for any loss or damage, whether consequential, incidental, special, or otherwise, that may result from the information presented in this book.

All images are free for use or purchased from stock photo sites or royalty-free for commercial use. I have relied on my own observations as well as many different sources for this book, and I have done my best to check facts and give credit where it is due. In the event that any material is used without proper permission, please contact me so that the oversight can be corrected.

The information provided in this book is for informational purposes only and is not intended to be a source of advice or credit analysis with respect to the material presented. The information and/or documents contained in this book do not constitute legal or financial advice and should never be used without first consulting with a financial professional to determine what may be best for your individual needs.

The publisher and the author do not make any guarantee or other promise as to any results that may be obtained from using the content of this book. You should never make any investment decision without first consulting with your own financial advisor and conducting your own research and due diligence. To the maximum extent permitted by law, the publisher and the author disclaim any and all liability in the event any information, commentary, analysis, opinions, advice and/or recommendations contained in this book prove to be inaccurate, incomplete or unreliable, or result in any investment or other losses.

Content contained or made available through this book is not intended to and does not constitute legal advice or investment advice and no attorney-client relationship is formed. The publisher and the author are providing this book and its contents on an "as is" basis. Your use of the information in this book is at your own risk.

TABLE OF CONTENTS.

TABLE OF CONTENTS. 3
INTRODUCTION. 5
CHAPTER 1 8
    Importance Of Financial Literacy For Teens. 8
CHAPTER 2 16
    How Teens Can Learn To Manage Credit Cards. 16
CHAPTER 3 26
    How to Assist Your Teenager in Comprehending Taxes. 26
CHAPTER 4 29
    Why Should Teens Begin Saving Early? 29
CHAPTER 5 33
    Part-Time Employment Opportunities For teenagers. 33
CHAPTER 6 40
    Ways Teenagers Can Generate Passive Income. 40
CHAPTER 7 47
    Maintain Your Paycheck by Raising a Financially Self-sufficient Teen. 47
CHAPTER 8 52
    Financial Attitudes To Help Your Teenager. 52
CHAPTER 9 56
    Preparing Teenagers For Financial Freedom. 56

CONCLUSION. 60

INTRODUCTION.

Regrettably, our educational system still trains us to behave like Victorians. They teach us arithmetic, English and a few other courses that will assist us daily. However, when it comes to financial education, most lectures are prehistoric.

They teach us to swap our time for money; they advise us to obtain employment and have a boss who tells us when to take a vacation and when to report to work, all for sometimes less than the minimum salary, not to mention paying additional tax. They punish us for making errors, and if we do not pass our examinations, we are considered failures.

You do not get into a good school by memorizing what a government bureaucrat tells you. In real life, individuals learn from their mistakes; similarly, financially educated individuals attempt to learn from the mistakes of others, which may end up being less costly for them.

For me, the most influential individuals are the youth, particularly teenagers. I believe it is important that we do not raise them with the same values as our parents. They must learn to be entrepreneurs, be creative, and use their creativity to generate revenue-generating ideas.

They must also learn how to make their money work for them. They are not pursuing a wage their entire lives with social security as their pot of gold at the end of the rainbow.

A guaranteed state pension or a mutual fund yields perhaps 100% in 15 years, even though the fuel price can climb 100% in a single year. How is this possible to be the financial security that job seekers aspire to?

This is a prescription for economic disaster, as many teens are unfamiliar with credit card and mortgage use fundamentals, despite nearly two decades of instruction in school and university.

To avoid this and other difficulties, we must continue to have education, but individuals must be competent to teach these subjects. If you want to learn how to make money, you must first learn from successful individuals.

If your financial advisor works in an office and earns $1000 per week selling life insurance to you or someone similar, how can he advise you on how to earn $1000,000 or, for that matter, show you how to make a million;

If he knew how to make a million, he would not be working in an office for $1000 a week or driving a BMW for $500 per month with a 15% interest rate.

If you want to give your teenager a leg up in life, teach them these skills immediately. This is the only way for them to achieve financial freedom.

Happy Reading

CHAPTER 1

Importance Of Financial Literacy For Teens.

Every parent knows that it is their responsibility to talk to our teens about 'sex' and 'drinking.' Opening up the doors of communication can help people make better judgments.

One topic that is still not talked about enough is 'money.' Consequently, young individuals have massive debt and credit troubles that will torment them through their late 20's and if not their entire lives.

You wouldn't give your sixteen-year-old the keys to your automobile without drivers' instruction, so don't let them move out without a practical financial education?

Both situations might damage your child's financial condition for years.

Young people are sent into the "real world" every day with disturbingly little knowledge of how to handle their finances. Even the tiniest mistakes can have a lasting impact on your child's financial destiny. Their credit history will be tarnished by a single missed credit card payment for seven years.

This could ultimately result in a downward spiral of financial calamities if they continue to make these blunders.

Public high schools are already well-known for their lack of practical financial instruction for teens. Those who are guardians or parents already know how important money management is for their children's stress levels, health, and overall quality of life.

That means that as parents, you must teach your children the financial literacy they will need in today's economy.

There are essential financial lessons you can teach your children. However, you must identify your teaching principles and approach before you do. Three prevalent parenting styles influence how your children view money.

- Parents who do not believe they are qualified. This is the most often encountered parental dilemma regarding giving practical financial education to children. These parents often experience stress because they recognize the important nature of financial education but are unsure where to begin.

They may lack confidence in training their children because they do not correctly comprehend financial problems. When their children begin to make the same financial mistakes they did, they often feel guilty.

If you identify with this situation, let go of any negative emotions, as it is not your fault. If you're like most individuals, you were also never taught this information. Therefore, use this opportunity to teach your children about money and grow together.

- Parents who are opposed to teaching. Many parents have a general awareness that money matters but are unsure how to teach their children. They're uncertain of what to teach, how to teach it, and whether their children will heed their counsel.

They also recognize that they may respond better to other persons imparting practical financial lessons throughout their children's teen years. As a parent, you are not responsible for teaching your children biology or geometry, so why should you feel obligated to teach them a subject as vital as money?

- Parents who enroll their child in the hard knocks school. Many of us have learned the hard way about money. Often, errors are made, forcing us to work even harder to correct them. Parents who believe in this learning method are taking a significant risk with their children's lives, one that could have catastrophic long-term effects.

There are options available to help your child get a financial start; make use of them! Often, the lessons learned in the school of hard knocks last a lifetime. However, these errors often destroy your child's confidence and eliminate all possibility of your youngster ever obtaining financial independence.

Each teenager should take a professional financial education course to escape the financial traps that plague so many people. The following are three suggestions to assist you in preparing your child for a structured financial education course.

1) Way of life. Children and teenagers are generally unconcerned with money. Money is what encourages them to learn. By associating money with leisure, freedom, and a way of life, they will be motivated to learn about money. Once they grasp the personal freedom that money provides, you'll find that your children become enthusiastic and eager to obtain a practical financial education.

Connecting money and lifestyle is an excellent way to get to know your children better, and it's also the first step toward assisting them in developing a good relationship with money. Take a moment to speak with them about their dreams.

Regardless of how improbable their financial aspirations appear to you, appreciate them and utilize them to drive them to study everything they can about financial matters.

For instance, if your sixteen-year-old dreams of one day owning a restaurant, ensure that you support his ambition. Rather than training children to save money for no purpose, you can now use their objective as an excuse to teach them about money matters.

2) Bank Accounts; They should open checking, savings, and investment accounts as soon as possible. It makes no difference if they are in kindergarten or college; setting up these accounts early will gain a lifetime advantage.

The longer your association with a bank or financial institution has been formed, the more benefits your child may enjoy. Most banks provide incentives to customers who have been with them longer than new customers do not enjoy. They provide preferred clients with different incentives, including lower rates, better terms, and more services, and they often qualify, for loans more easily.

Along with the financial benefits, teenagers who have the correct accounts open feel more responsible for their financial future. This sense of responsibility is important for adequately preparing your child before they move out to live independently.

3) Make an early investment. Encourage your teen to begin investing once they have saved up some money. The stock market is an excellent location for children to begin; however, they should refrain from purchasing individual stocks or mutual funds. Both are excessively dangerous unless you have received specialist investment training. Alternatively, you might invest in the broader market.

Various investment vehicles make it as simple as purchasing a stock or mutual fund to invest in the general market. Making a simple market investment may provide your youngster with lower risk, more consistent returns, and increased diversification.

The best aspect is that this method is quite simple to implement. Once they've established their investing account, they can automate it so that the investment is made for them automatically each month.

Preparing your teen for the realities of the twenty-first century is an important aspect of responsible parenting. You would never give your child a car without first teaching them how to drive; similarly, before they move out, ensure they receive a real financial education. Providing them with real financial education before they move out on their own will benefit them for the rest of their lives.

CHAPTER 2

How Teens Can Learn To Manage Credit Cards.

The number of teenagers who own credit cards has risen dramatically. This has become a growing epidemic, with the majority of teenagers accruing significant debt. Due to their youth, most teenagers have no idea or understanding of debt management, and once they accumulate substantial amounts of debt, they have no idea how to get out of it.

As a result, most of them begin their lives with a bankruptcy or a poor credit history. The majority of them work extremely long hours but still fail to pay off their debts, and some even become trapped in circular debt crises in an attempt to pay off their debts.

Despite the overwhelmingly negative consequences, we will attempt to explain why there has been such a dramatic increase in teenager credit card debt.

This increase is due to the aggressive marketing by credit card companies and the myth that providing a credit card to a young child teaches them about money and debt management.

Also, credit card debt is viewed by teenagers as an extension of their income and freedom, allowing them to make purchases without bothering their parents or worrying about money. Finally, it is due to teens' ignorance of how credit cards work and the relationship between credit cards and cash. However, this lesson is learned, albeit the hard way.

Banks and credit card companies view students as potential customers and actively market to them today. Thus, when they begin their careers, the company will already have them as consumers. This results in additional revenue for the business.

Thus, they present the credit card as a necessary item for the student. Due to the influence of marketers, every student desires to appear cool, spend carelessly, and be free of cash and financing concerns. This liberty comes with a price, which the student is entirely unaware of.

Teenagers in high school or early college are too immature to be truly frugal with their spending. Many youngsters have many things vying for their attention, making it highly appealing to spend freely on whatever they want.

As a result, they continue to waste money on frivolous activities like going to the movies, drinking with friends, and ordering midnight pizzas. Meanwhile, they amass mountains of debt. Even consumer advocacy groups have expressed reservations about the legitimacy of handing a credit card to adolescents.

This implies they will have unrestricted access to online items that are not acceptable for them, such as pornographic content, harmful liquors, and lethal weapons that can be acquired online without their parent's knowledge using a credit card.

Parents feel that providing their teens with a credit card will educate them to be responsible, but this is not the case. Teenagers perceive it as free money and are generally unaware of the interest, late fees, and other expenses involved with non-payment.

When the credit card gets unmanageable, parents typically pitch in to rescue their child, making them even more irresponsible with the payment because they know they will be rescued soon.

Recent surveys indicate that only 52% of high school kids are aware of credit card and tax difficulties, indicating a dire situation. These are the students who marketers are after, and their ignorance makes them vulnerable.

Teens who are unable to pay off their financial debt eventually ruin their credit history. Some even commit suicide due to their unmanageable debt and the lack of assistance.

You must teach your teenagers the value of money, but they also require some form of card or cash to begin their independence. If you're not sure which type of credit card is best for your children, here's some guidance on credit cards for teenagers.

Avoid using a standard credit card.

If you have children, you should avoid traditional credit cards, as they do not encourage responsible spending. While a credit card enables a child to make spending mistakes and learn from them, simply providing them with a line of credit will almost certainly result in disaster. You have no way of preventing them from spending the entire limit in one go, which puts you and your family in debt.

Cards prepaid.

Despite the fact that traditional credit cards are a bad idea, there is a new type of card on the market specifically for children.

These cards, dubbed prepaid cards, have the majority of the features of a credit card, with the exception that you load money onto the card in the same way you would a mobile phone. Rather than giving your child a credit card, you can load money onto the card each week or month and let them use it as they please.

Prepaid cards have a number of advantages.

The primary advantage of a prepaid card is that it combines the convenience of having a card with the ability to manage spending. This makes it essential for parents who want to instill financial responsibility in their children while still maintaining control over how much and on what they spend.

By providing their child with a card that includes a statement, the parent can monitor how and when their child spends their money. This is an extremely useful tool for educating children about money management. Additionally, prepaid cards are safer than having your child carry cash, enabling them to make internet purchases.

Prepaid card disadvantages.

While many believe these cards are safer for children than other financial products, there are still concerns about their viability. Although they are marketed as a tool to teach youngsters about money, this can be accomplished in a variety of ways other than by handing them a card.

Additionally, keeping track of spending is not always straightforward, as some cards allow cash withdrawals, allowing users to spend their money on anything. Additionally, there is a risk that parents will load the cards with too much money, which will have the reverse effect of teaching children about money and would lead them to feel they can spend everything they want.

Additionally, these cards have expenses associated with them, such as an application fee and top-up fees. While these cards may be beneficial for certain families, you should carefully consider the benefits and drawbacks before deciding whether or not to give your child one.

Consider the link that exists between students and their credit cards. One widespread assumption we all appear to believe is that no student can manage his or her funds.

We think that simply because someone is still a teenager, they lack the discipline necessary to rein down their expenditures. Is that a fair representation of the millions of students who populate our world? I have my doubts. In my interactions with younger individuals, I've discovered that many are well-adjusted and can manage their finances well.

Naturally, not all children are truly prepared for the big scary world of credit cards. That does take some getting used to. There is a lot of jargon that must be grasped initially. There are a plethora of rules that must be observed. There are a plethora of monthly payments that must be paid.

Also, there is the tremendous convenience with which a credit card enables you to manage your many expenses. Once you leave the security of your home and move to campus, the newfound freedom can feel incredible. However, this newly acquired freedom from restraints might lead to a totally another way of life and excessive spending.

College is a wholly unique experience. It might be pretty shocking if you are unprepared, and credit cards are among the variables that contribute to this life's novelty.

That is why an increasing number of institutions emphasize the relevance of credit card usage among their students, and colleges are not alone in this regard. Credit card issuers have likewise agreed to drop the term "opportunistic." They, too, have developed courses (some of which are certified) to educate young pupils about the various facets of credit usage.

Many teenagers act as if credit cards are free money. Many financial education courses educate teenagers about the advantages and disadvantages of credit cards. A college student can maximize credit card rewards by prudently using the card.

Credit card debt can result from irresponsible credit card usage. Students should be aware of this risk before developing a habit of budgeting excessively. Credit history can stalk an individual for years. However, you can avoid this by playing your cards prudently.

CHAPTER 3

How to Assist Your Teenager in Comprehending Taxes.

Teenagers tend to take life extremely literally. For instance, when teenagers accept a job, they expect to earn the exact amount offered. However, life doesn't work that way, and you can help your teenager adjust by teaching them about taxes.

Everyone, regardless of income, is subject to income tax. The government can generate funds through these taxes to provide citizens with beneficial services and military fund efforts.

Your teen must understand that calculating their weekly income hourly is not an exact science. Explaining how income taxes operate will help them understand that their hourly wage is a rough estimate of how much they earned during a day of work. The number of hours they work multiplied by their hourly salary will not equal the amount they see on their cheque.

When a teen obtains employment, they will be required to complete a tax form that they are unlikely to comprehend. Tax forms must be completed accurately, as the government will use this information to determine the amount and type of taxes to deduct from their paycheck. As a result, parents must assist their teens in comprehending the details of tax forms and filling them out.

Individuals who earn less than a government-specified sum are not obligated to file taxes. The majority of youths who work fall under this category and are tax-exempt, particularly in their first year of employment.

Parents should assist their children in increasing their incomes by claiming all available tax deductions. For instance, being included on your parents' tax returns is a tax deduction that allows them to retain a greater portion of the money they have worked so hard to earn. This is an excellent decision, as the majority of teenagers will not be filing their taxes.

As teenagers mature and begin to earn more money, their approach to taxation will evolve. Assist them in understanding that they should do all possible to take advantage of the brief period during which they will not be taxed, as this will not be the case once they earn more money and are required to file for and pay further taxes.

Many teenagers generate money independently by selling items on eBay, babysitting, and performing other tasks. These profits may bring your teen's income up to the point where they must file taxes.

You can determine your eligibility for avoiding filing taxes. Also, it might be prudent to explain some of the many tax forms to your child and encourage them to preserve money, as they may owe the IRS taxes.

Teaching kids about taxes from the start of their working lives will prepare them to deal with this reality. Discuss with them the importance of keeping accurate records of their earnings so that they can determine whether or not the government compels them to submit taxes at the end of the year.

CHAPTER 4

Why Should Teens Begin Saving Early?

What if the best financial present you ever gave a child costs you nothing but results in them inheriting a million - or a two-dollar nest egg?

If you're the frugal type, that should put a grin on your face. Therefore, what is this magnificent financial gift?

Of course, advise. This is to say that if one begins saving regularly as a child, the amount of money that may be acquired over a substantial length of time is astounding.

The amount of money a person earns determines their wealth; the amount of money they save and the earlier they begin, the better.

When an individual's investment income exceeds their monthly expenses, he or she has achieved financial independence. Numerous people who appear wealthy earn substantial salaries but have little or no net worth; they may also be deeply in debt and far from financially self-sufficient."

"Financial experts agree that it is critical to begin teaching children about money at an early age, as early as age 5 or 6, or at the very least well before they begin using credit cards and mobile apps. By the time we reach the age of seven, our attitudes toward money are largely formed through imitation of our parents' behavior."

"Assume you begin investing $2000 per year at the age of 19 and stop at 29 (a total of ten years) for a total investment of $22,000, while your brother begins investing $2000 per year at the age of 38 and continues until he is 60 (a total of twenty-two years for a total investment of $46,000). Assuming a 6.5 percent annual return, you'll have more than $231,000 in your portfolio by the time you reach 60, while your brother would have around $ "7,000,000."

In other words, compound interest requires time to work its magic.

However, money is the most lovely part - not all of it. Indeed, far more critical than the amount of money saved is adopting the practice of saving money aside regularly, i.e., paying yourself first.

Pay yourself first - and you will achieve financial security.

How much should you pay yourself?

Consider the following additional figures;

"How much money do you think you'd end up with if you invested $2400 every year, say $200 per month, over the following 30 years and averaged a 15% annual return?"

1.4 million dollars. Wow!

However, for all the teenagers out there, consider this: "If you start saving $30 a month at the age of 18 and continue until you are 65 (or 47 years), earning an average of 15% per year, how much would you finish up with?"

Two million dollars. WOW!

"Among the primary reasons saving is so tough is that no one truly wants you to. That is true. Everybody wants you to spend as much money as possible."

CHAPTER 5

Part-Time Employment Opportunities For teenagers.

You've just turned sixteen and are feeling rather confident about yourself. You recently obtained your driver's license and, with the assistance of your parents, purchased your first automobile, which enables you to travel and do things alone that you were never able to do as a 15-year-old.

You have the flexibility to drive yourself to parties, school dances and high school football games, and the cinema or the beach with your date. The trouble is, now that you have more responsibilities such as car payments, you must also begin earning more money than you did last year.

This is why you should seek a higher-paying position, and in this post, we'll point you in the direction of the finest part-time jobs for 16-year-olds so you can begin paying off your car and save some money. Although these are difficult economic times, there are still some highly well-paying employment available.

A waiter or waitress is among the best part-time professions available to a 16-year-old. Waitersing positions are among the highest paying professions available to teenagers, and this is not due to the hourly income, which typically ranges between $9 and $13 per hour. This is due to the suggestions you can make over there. If a waitress or waiter is competent, she or he can often earn between $100 and $200 in tips.

When people enter a restaurant to dine, they are searching for a decent meal, but they are also looking for someone with whom to converse and who may make them feel a bit better than they did when they entered. Thus, your role is not just to deliver exceptional culinary service to these customers but also to act as a psychologist by catering to their needs for self-esteem.

A good waiter or waitress can quickly establish a reputation among the restaurant's patrons, and if you are widely loved, patrons will often request to sit at the table where you are waitersing. It's a fast-paced environment, and you'll need much energy to succeed.

If a waiting job is a little too fast-paced for you, I would consider applying for a librarian position at your local library. Librarians often earn between $8 and $12 per hour, but they work many off-hours, which gives you plenty of time not only to read your favorite books but also to focus on your homework and complete it so that you can have fun and hang out with friends when you get home.

If your day is far too stressful for you, volunteering at your local library may be the answer to your prayers. By the time you stop working at your favorite library, you will have gained expertise in different disciplines due to enough time you will have to study many books.

Babysitting is the most prevalent employment for teenagers aged 14 and up. This is the most secure position for them, as their sole responsibility will be to care for a child on behalf of its parents. Almost every teenager has had their experience babysitting.

The second most popular option is to work as a diner server in restaurants and fast-food chains, which can be extremely rewarding, particularly if the establishment is packed with generous clients leaving large tips daily.

Typically, we see teenagers and students working as food servers in burger stands or coffee shops. This type of job is beneficial for teenagers since it enables them to earn money to help finance their education. However, there are still many job options for students and teenagers that will allow them to make money while simultaneously preparing them for a future career.

Some of the best occupations for young people, such as students and teenagers, expose them to the possibilities of a professional career. For instance, if students and teens aspire to be teachers in the future, they can seek employment as tutors for younger students or weaker students in a certain subject topic.

Also, some youngsters who aspire to be successful businessmen can obtain summer jobs as assistants or secretaries in businesses. By securing this type of work, teenagers will be able to develop simple grasps that will aid them in comprehending business operations.

Some hospitals also provide jobs in health care for teenagers. Students and teenagers are encouraged to apply for part-time positions at hospitals, clinics, and other health care service facilities.

They will be able to learn a few things while working here that will help them in the future if they wish to become nurses, medical technologists, or doctors, or other vocations in the fields of medicine and health care.

Teenagers typically seek for enjoyable careers. This is why people require occupations that align with their passions and interests. If you are a teenager with a passion for animals and pets, working in a local zoo or animal clinic as a part-time or full-time employee will be an excellent option for you.

This allows teenagers to learn more about the subjects they are enthusiastic about. Working in a store that offers automobiles, motorcycles, and other vehicles for youngsters interested in autos may be the best option.

Teenagers are typically quite impulsive and want to try a variety of activities simultaneously. They are easily bored, even more so when they are working. This is why parents should consider finding them a job that allows them to have fun while earning money and learning from their experience.

However, careers are ideal for teenagers that do not involve backbreaking work or long hours standing and performing repetitive tasks without earning much money. Online jobs suited for 14-year-old teenagers range from blogging and responding to internet survey forms. These jobs are undoubtedly the easiest and most financially rewarding jobs for 14+ youngsters.

The youngster will be compensated based on the number of completed online survey questionnaires. The work schedule is flexible and their efforts are measured in terms of completed questionnaires. All they require is a personal computer or laptop with continuous internet access.

If they prefer to postpone their work for the day, they do so freely, unlike other physical vocations that need adherence to a strict timetable each day. Online employment like this can be considered safe because they allow employees to work from the comfort of their homes and do not need them to commute.

CHAPTER 6

Ways Teenagers Can Generate Passive Income.

Online Earning Opportunities for Teens

You may be unaware, but there are hundreds of methods to earn money online. Because most teenagers currently hunt for work online, job postings and random Internet assignments are increasing.

It demonstrates teens' ongoing pursuit of financial independence, and the World Wide Web is unquestionably, the finest location for teenagers to earn money, as earning online opportunities are convenient and free.

Teens can do a lot online. If they possess particular expertise, such as writing, web design, or programming, they can fully utilize it online.

Freelance work online is among the most popular ways for kids to make money quickly.

Internet marketing is particularly popular today, which means that writing random articles for writing service providers could potentially work as long-term employment. As long as you can write high-quality articles quickly, you can earn $20-$25 in about 2 to 3 hours.

This income could further increase if you concentrate on articles about health, finance, and investing, as these are the most lucrative sectors. Teenagers may also participate in affiliate marketing. They might earn up to $15 by simply supplying names, surnames, residences, states, and zip codes.

If you are still dissatisfied with these methods, you can get additional information on making money gadgets area growing patient sites. These websites provide additional information on how to earn money online.

Through the use of a digital camera.

Thanks to the information age and some creative thinking, the rapidly expanding number of teens can sustain themselves with a comfortable passive income. Their one-of-a-kind gadget is a simple digital camera.

It is a well-known fact that job employment is not the most secure option in today's globalized globe. Social security, on the other hand, does not. Individuals discover that even if they work for a "blue-chip firm," their futures are not bright as previous generations.

Businesses are laying off employees and outsourcing work to countries with lower labor. They let their twenty- and thirty-year staff become unemployed. Companies are slashing benefits and reducing contributions to existing employees.

The information era has made teenagers aware of global events. Their parents, uncles, and neighbors are losing jobs at large corporations. Teenagers whose parents are still employed recognize that they will be unable to spend meaningful time together.

These teens consider alternate ways to live a pleasant existence without sacrificing money, family, or time. They discovered the simple solution: passive income is living a comfortable life without compromising money, family, or leisure.

The cost of a digital camera, a computer, and an internet connection decreases. The internet is a free marketplace where anyone can sell digital products to anyone else on the earth. The purchaser makes a credit card purchase and downloads the product. The business no longer incurs shipping costs.

Some individuals post their digital photographs online and are compensated for them. Teenagers feel the same way. Submitting photographs to stock picture sites does not require the photographer to be a professional. The two most important pieces of equipment are a digital camera and an internet connection.

Businesses and people often utilize stock photo sites since it is less expensive to browse through the stock photo sites for what they need than to hire a professional photographer, which could wind up costing more. They earn more money the more digital images they upload.

This is an excellent opportunity for anyone with a digital camera to earn a comfortable living online. Some businesses want images daily online and are looking for individuals to give these photos in exchange for an hourly payment based on the number of hours spent uploading those photos; no expertise is necessary to begin earning money using a digital camera.

Flipping Houses.

Flipping houses can be an excellent strategy to quickly earn a substantial sum of money. Whatever your age, if you have the knowledge and ability to flip a house, you could be well on your way to a huge cash account. Consider this: if you can learn to flip properties at an early age, you can begin establishing your financial independence one flipped house at a time.

The real estate market is constantly in a state of flux. At one time, the cycle is at a low point, allowing you to purchase houses at rock bottom prices, and the cycle reaches a peak, allowing you to sell the property for more than you anticipated.

Because flipping properties requires little or no money down, it may be the ideal career for the younger generation. Attend a meeting with your teenager at a program or group specializing in educating individuals on how to flip houses.

Allow them to witness firsthand the endless income flow that comes with flipping houses. Getting your teen excited about this could be among the most beneficial things you ever do for them in the actual world.

If you want to take your assistance a step further, why not help them flip their first couple of houses? Learning together is an excellent approach to alleviate some of the tension associated with the first time.

To stay ahead of the curve in today's society, you must have the inside scoop. You could be the one who delivers such a scoop to your child, giving people the ability to invest money in the house flipping business and a sense of satisfaction and pride when their properties are sold. Nothing is more gratifying than knowing that you have a say in your financial independence, especially when still in your teen years.

CHAPTER 7

Maintain Your Paycheck by Raising a Financially Self-sufficient Teen.

It is more important than ever for parents to arm their teens with the knowledge necessary to navigate the real financial world in today's environment. Young people confront financial difficulties the moment they leave the safety net of their parents.

Every day, we read about the consequences of people being unprepared: record debt, foreclosures, and bankruptcies are just a few of the issues people face. These are the major ones but keep in mind that a single late credit card payment will hound them for seven years. If you provide your children with the fundamental financial education skills necessary for financial independence, these issues can be avoided.

By examining the statistics, it is clear that most parents lack the knowledge necessary to educate a financially responsible teen. For the last 50 years, public high schools have taught similar subjects, but financial education is not among them. As a result, many parents were never taught about money and are ill-equipped to raise a financially responsible teen.

Raising a financially responsible teen is crucial in today's world. You may use strategies to prepare your child for financial independence at an early age. Even if you have made financial mistakes, there are options available to assist you in providing your children with the advantages that many parents desire.

Assisting your high school or college-aged child in achieving financial independence will provide them with an advantage they will use daily.

Developing a strong moral character will enable your youngster to earn more money, be a more competitive job prospect and be an all-around respectable person. Being a well-respected member of the community will assist them in achieving financial independence in today's society. The wealthiest and most respected individuals are those who uphold high ethical standards.

The key to raising a financially responsible teen is to develop their communication abilities. It endows them to persuade others and align them with their personal goals, a necessary quality for increased earning power.

Assisting them in developing their writing and speaking skills increases their chances of being employed and ensures they are paid fairly. Also, exceptional communicators are more likely to be promoted to leadership positions or become successful entrepreneurs.

Negativity impedes many aspects of life and can jeopardize a teenager's chances of financial independence. Teach your children to think strategically.

Creating a vivid image of their desired outcome will provide them with the drive necessary to accomplish their goals. Favorable attitudes attract positive events, so encourage them to cultivate a mindset that will assist them in maturing into a happy, well-rounded, financially responsible adult.

Assist your teen in identifying and pursuing their passions. Provide them with guidance on how to earn money by following their passions. When your child is passionate about their work, it ceases to feel like work, and they thrive at it. By knowing your teen's dreams, you will gain a better knowledge of them and assist them in developing a life-long skill.

Having solid organizational habits would aid in achieving financial independence at an early age. Set an example; demonstrate to your teen child the benefits of having an organized schedule, space, and life. This will enable them to maximize their earning potential.

These steps can help you get started on the path to financial independence. Of course, extra financial lessons must be given to assist them in managing their money; nevertheless, assisting your kid in developing a sound mind is a key first step.

By assisting them in developing these skills, you are assisting them in gaining the freedom associated with not having to worry about money. You may assist your child in attaining financial independence at an early age by equipping them with the required skills to succeed in the real world.

CHAPTER 8

Financial Attitudes To Help Your Teenager.

Teenagers and money are two mutually exclusive words. The former typically seeks and requires the latter. As a parent during these shifting financial times, what can you advise your adolescent about money?

Besides the fact that it does not grow on trees? As parents, we all want our children to grow up to be responsible adults and financially successful ones. Here are 7 financial mindsets that can benefit your adolescent.

1. Expect fluctuation.

If there is a particular lesson we can take from history and money, there is volatility. Just as sure as there are good economic times, there are poor economic ones. Economics may be as unpredictable as the weather and equally as frustrating if you let it.

2. Nothing compares to a dollar earned.

Your parents' money is not necessarily your money. While it may seem like having money delivered to you whenever you want is a dream, something is rewarding about earning it yourself. The work equity you have spent in your income can never compare to the mediocrity of a handout.

3. Keep in mind to save.

Just as money fluctuates, life does as well. Everybody encounters financial difficulties and unanticipated difficulties on occasion. As a result, it is necessary to have some form of savings to fall back on to alleviate stress. Also, saving enables you to avoid incurring credit card debt.

4. Credit accrues to you.

Credit must be handled wisely. Your credit score determines your eligibility for credit cards, payment plans, and loans. Your credit actions today will directly affect your future financial capability.

Even some employers will take a person's credit history into account when recruiting an employee.

5. Put it to work.

Not only is it critical to manage money responsibly, but also wisely. You work hard for your money; why not make it work for you? There are many investment prospects. Self-education is necessary, as is seeking the advice of a skilled financial practitioner.

6. Do not be frightened to use it prudently.

Saving money is a wonderful thing. Investing is also beneficial. Money, on the other hand, is designed to be enjoyed. The trick is to spend it prudently and responsibly.

7. Do not make it the basis of your self-identity.

As humans, we naturally tend to regard affluent folks with a greater degree of esteem than others. Financial prosperity can be seductive. It can make a person feel strong, popular, and significant.

However, there is a problem when an individual puts his or her inner worth on money.

Why?

Apart from the fact that it fluctuates, there will always be someone with more money than you. Or perhaps it has increased its investment, etc. Self-identity must be derived from one's inner character, not from one's external financial situation.

As teenagers mature, they must learn essential life lessons. As a parent, instilling healthy financial attitudes in your teenager can profoundly affect their relationship with money.

CHAPTER 9

Preparing Teenagers For Financial Freedom.

Adulthood is only a few short years away for high school kids, and with it, the financial freedom to sign leases, take out loans and charge to credit cards. Because many teenagers lack the patience for lengthy financial discussions, prioritize the following chores and discussion topics.

1. Assist in the establishment of a checking account. In most states, children above the age of 13 can open a checking account with the signature of a parent or guardian.

If you consider opening an account, take your children to the bank and sit down with a banker who can explain how to deposit and withdraw money, use a debit card, and the consequences of an overdraft. Having a checking account teaches your kids about banking and makes it easier for them to manage their own money if they have a job, a car, or other financial responsibilities.

2. If possible, encourage part-time work. Each child is unique, and while some teens are ready to begin working as soon as they are able, others may want assistance in discovering suitable possibilities. If your children often ask for money for petrol, clothing or other discretionary items, part-time work may be an excellent choice.

However, ensure that your children consistently emphasize schoolwork and other important extracurricular activities. A part-time job can help teenagers develop a work ethic, make new friends and professional contacts, and earn extra money.

3. Discuss how to pay for college. Whether you plan to pay for your children's school or expect them to save their money and take out student loans, it's important to discuss college economics. Establishing financial expectations for higher education far in

advance of your children filling out college applications is important.

The more time your children have to apply for scholarships and save a portion of their allowance or earnings from a part-time job, the better. If you want to pay for your children's tuition, be candid about your financial situation and the expenses (if any) you will be unable to cover, such as room and board or textbooks.

4. Encourage the establishment of financial goals. If your teen receives an allowance or a monthly wage, propose they set two or three financial objectives for themselves before graduation.

Whether they're saving for college, a down payment on a used car, or a gaming console, learning to set and track financial goals will help them grasp the fundamentals of money management.

Keep in mind that healthy money habits may be taught with the appropriate amount of financial support and freedom. High school is the ideal time for your children to begin accepting real budgetary obligations and develop a sense of comfort with them before the financial strains of college set in.

CONCLUSION.

Nowadays, life is more difficult, and practically everyone faces challenges and financial difficulties. It's reassuring to know that there are occupations for teenagers that can help them maintain themselves financially.

Previously, people believed that there was no employment for teenagers due to their lack of experience and lower motivation to work. However, various paying occupations are available for teenagers who are ready to earn money to help with their expenses at school or home.

Teenagers often work as crew in fast food restaurants. Teenagers may easily apply for and are approved into this profession because it takes only a few basic skills such as serving and cleaning. However, some youths cannot perform all these chores, which can be time-consuming and drain their energy and strength.

We are all aware that this type of work entails long hours. This is among the disadvantages of working as a crew member in fast food restaurants. This is also why kids would like to choose another profession that does not need much work but still allows them to earn money.

If you believe you are among the youngsters who struggle to find that type of employment, then perhaps jobs for teenagers online are the perfect option for you.

Many youngsters are looking for employment online since, aside from the comfort of working from home, the compensation is relatively high compared to jobs that demand much time and energy. Many businesses hire writers to provide material for their websites or blogs.

If you have a passion for writing, this is an excellent opportunity. Apart from writing, another popular online profession where you can earn a good living is survey taking. Many websites offer extremely lucrative compensation for completing survey questionnaires.

What is required of you is to conduct an online search for a reputable paid web survey company, register, and provide your personal information. After they accept your accounts, you will receive your first survey and be paid according to the agreed-upon terms and conditions.

However, these are not the only employment for teenagers available online. Plenty of jobs match your interests. Working online is among the most convenient and lucrative careers available to teenagers. It will empower children to manage their own time and instill a feeling of responsibility, preparing them for life in the real world as they get older.

Series: Financial Freedom at Any Age

- Achieving Financial Freedom in your 20's
- Achieving Financial Freedom in your 30's
- Achieving Financial Freedom in your 40's
- Achieving Financial Freedom in your 50's
- Achieving Financial Freedom in your 60's
- Achieving Financial Freedom in your 70's and beyond.
- Achieving Financial Freedom in children
- Achieving Financial Freedom in teenagers
- Achieving Financial Freedom in college students.
- Financial Scams to be Aware of in Retirement.

www.ingramcontent.com/pod-product-compliance
Lightning Source LLC
Chambersburg PA
CBHW040324220526
45473CB00009B/2558